Don't Come In Here! Mom's Throwing Spaghetti!

Don't Come In Here! Mom's Throwing Spaghetti!

Renee Hawkley

PENNINGTON PUBLISHING

BOISE, IDAHO

Don't Come In Here! Mom's Throwing Spaghetti!
2nd Edition

Copyright © 2000 by Renee Hawkley

Library of Congress Card Number: 00-190626

ISBN 0-9665177-0-9

Acknowledgments

I express my sincere love and appreciation to:

- *my husband, Dan, who shares tears of joy and anxiety with me as we strive to be capable parents.*

- *my children, Danny, Jill, Curtis, Clayton, Kyle, Anthony, Ethan, and Janette, who make every day an adventure and allow me to tell their stories.*

- *my grandchildren, Rachel and Charles, who love their grandparents "mucher and mucher."*

- *my friends and neighbors who contribute immeasurably to my family.*

Note to Reader

This booklet is comprised of articles written over the period of several years. They do not appear in the order in which they were written. Each article has been previously published in newspapers, magazines or books.

"Dear Renee,
I get the idea you enjoy what you're doing.
Keep doing it."

Erma Bombeck

"Some time ago, I cut 'Graduation Day' from the Reader's Digest, written by you. I have four grandsons whose rooms are a total disaster, exactly as you described. Can you please send me this article so that I can frame it to give to my daughter?"

Anne Lorraine, Palm Beach, Flórida

"I have been receiving 'Welcome Home' for years and I just love it. I always search for an article by you and if there is one, read it first. You are my favorite 'Welcome Home' author."

Kathy Rothermich, Wentzville, Missouri

"Thank you for your wonderful outlook on parenting. A friend of mine allowed me to read her copy of 'Don't Come In Here!....' I smiled and laughed on every page. On a few pages I cried."

Kate Larkin, Boise, Idaho

"Thank you for your article on teenage boys. I highlighted it, cut it out and hung it on the fridge as a daily reminder."

Jennifer Christ, Milwaukee, Wisconsin

"I was beginning to think I or the boys needed counseling before I read your article."

Janet Dittmer, Vienna, Virginia

"We want to thank you for sharing your experiences of mothering with us. Your insight and humor were both encouraging and refreshing. We all left with some new ideas and a new friend."

Karen Patterson, Boise, Idaho

Table of Contents

About the Author

Renee is the mother of six boys and two girls. She writes a family-life column using empathy and humor to communicate a message of encouragement to other mothers. Renee is also a motivational speaker with a message tailored to women's groups and interfaith gatherings.

After enjoying 29 years as a stay-at-home-mom, Renee is presently the librarian at Lowell Scott Middle School, where she serves as a catalyst for success to many students acquiring a love of reading.

She lives with her family in Boise, Idaho and was named Idaho's Mother of the Year 2000.

Renee's email address is

reneehawkley@rmci.net

or you can find her at

www.idahomom.com

Her mailing address is:

10490 Treeline Street
Boise, Idaho 83704

She would love to hear from you.

About the Illustrator

The cover illustration was done by Renee's niece, Kim Mickelson. At the time of this publication, Kim is a student at Utah State University, where she studies art. Her talents include sculpting, pottery and illustration.

This booklet is dedicated

to my mom and dad,

William
&
Verla Thomas,

who inspired me
with the desire to be a mother.

"Isn't My Mother Beautiful Today?"

Since I was young, my dad often asked his children a familiar question. "Isn't your mother beautiful today?" Of course, we always nodded in agreement, but sometimes, we children shared quick glances of bewilderment after his question.

Our mother didn't wear makeup or fancy clothes. She combed her hair like a lot of other women in our small Idaho community, and I didn't hear anybody calling THEM beautiful. I wondered whether my dad was aware of the pretty women on the cover of *Life* magazine. I couldn't imagine my mother wearing a bathing suit in a beauty pageant, and even if she did, I didn't think her figure would attract much of a following. It was a puzzle to me.

After I left home and began experiencing life on the other side of childhood, I started to notice features about my mother that I had never noticed as a child. Year after year, her beauty steadily increased to its present radiance.

She has the ability to light up a room by walking into it. Her hair is so white, it glistens, and it crowns her delicate face like a halo. Her beauty is like a people magnet. It's common for total strangers to approach her from across a crowded room to give her a compliment or a hug. Her numerous friends and family still benefit from daily acts of service performed by her busy, gentle hands.

My mother's captivating brown eyes are the best ears on the planet. They listen to every syllable you say. They are usually focused on completing a beloved task, following the words and actions of a loved one, sparkling with pride or shedding tender tears of empathy and love. My mother's beautiful, brown eyes have actually performed miracles in my life many times.

My mother turned 86 years old on March 2nd, 2000. If only you could meet her. Then, I would turn to you and ask, "Isn't my mother beautiful today?"

don't come in
here!
Mom's throwing
spagetti!

The Evolution of
A Parent

Once upon a time, I knew exactly how to raise children. After all, I was a college junior majoring in child development. I had organized all the parenting questions and answers in a fat, black binder. That was before I learned that with parenthood, you start out knowing all the answers and few of the questions and move steadily toward knowing all the questions and few of the answers.

I got the first hint that my fat, black binder wasn't going to be my ticket to parenting success when a buxom nurse sauntered toward my hospital bed with a little blue bundle in her arms. "Here's your baby," she said, as she casually shifted the entire eight pounds and three ounces of brand-new human being from her arms to mine with a look that told me she thought I knew what to do with it. Here's your baby . . . three little words that formally ended my own childhood and began my child's.

All of a sudden, my fat, black binder didn't fit. It was crammed with flat words on flat pages. Everything in the little blue bundle was round . . . round head . . . round tummy . . . round fingers . . . and round eyes fastened on my own. I wondered what the round brain behind them was wondering. I was holding the very miracle of life, and that miracle

4

was totally dependent on me. Then came the question. "What do I do now?"

Seven bundle-deliveries later, I'm still asking the question. What do I do now? For every answer I toss away, at least two new questions boomerang back.

Maybe you can help. When a toddler eats a clump of soggy cat food, do we call poison control or just mop up her face? Why would a child rather play kick-the-can in the street than on expensive jungle gym equipment in his backyard? Why is grounding a teenager worse punishment for the parents than it is for the teenager? How can two children raised by the same parents be SO different? Where do you go to learn how to let go? When do you stop worrying? What do you tell a five-year-old who wants to run away from home? What do you tell a sixteen-year-old who wants to run away from home? What do you tell yourself when YOU want to run away from home?

The answers to at least a galaxy of other questions aren't addressed in my fat, black binder. That's because fat, black binders and parenting manuals are assembled by idealistic students and psychologists who wear pencils behind their ears and work behind desks in an environment where human behavior is somewhat predictable.

I keep my fat, black binder stored in a memory box and dig it out sometimes when I feel like recalling college memories of blissful innocence. Those were the days . . . when I thought all parenting questions could be answered on a pop quiz.

Who's In Charge Here?

A two-year-old child is like a piece of pie a la mode. It can be heaven on earth when you give it your full attention, but better not get distracted. If you do, there's going to be a puddle.

Because of two-year-olds, we have phrases like "accident waiting to happen," "a surprise a minute" and "sweet and sour." When a two-year-old bubble of joy throws chubby arms around your neck and then bursts in your lap by stamping a slobbery Vanilla Wafer kiss on your cheek, you have experienced "both the thrill of victory and the agony of defeat" in five seconds flat.

Parents and two-year-olds are like gerbils on an exercise wheel. Nobody keeps track of who got on first, where and why they're going, who's chasing who or, for that matter, who's ahead. They only know they had better stay on the wheel and keep running as fast as they can or they lose.

Having a two-year-old is the beginning of choosing up sides for the generation gap. Each side is attempting to establish an answer to the question, "Who's in charge here?"

A two-year-old child wants independence. He likes to feed himself. The "I do myself!" routine works well for peanut butter and jelly sandwiches and Cheerios. However, it gets complicated when it comes to ice cream sundaes and pork chops. Parents may think they deserve a "thank you" for their help. Instead, they are met with screams of, "Mine! Mine!" at the first hint of assistance.

A two-year-old doesn't agree with bedtime. He will not tolerate use of the words, "bed" or "nap" in his presence. That's when the spelling starts. One parent turns to the other and says, "I'm going to put Johnny down for his n-a-p now. Would you grab his b-l-a-n-k-i-e out of the dryer?"

A two-year-old child wants to dress herself. She wants to button the buttons, snap the snaps, pull on the shirts and tie the shoes. When some of these tasks are a bit beyond her ability, who gets the blame? The parents, of course.

A two-year-old child knows what he wants, and he wants it now. He wants to go in the car, but he doesn't want to be buckled into his car seat. She wants to hear the whole story, but she refuses to turn the pages one at a time. She wants to try her hand with crayons, but she prefers to have her work displayed on walls than on paper.

He wants to climb ON the counters and OFF the potty. She wants to throw toys IN to the puddle and OUT of the bathtub. He wants to be carried UP stairs when he's tired but not DOWN when you have a deadline to meet.

He wants to touch steaming food, but he doesn't want a bandaged finger. She wants to chase a bee, but she doesn't want the bee to chase her.

Two-year-olds are great teachers. They make parents younger . . . and older.

If you hadn't learned it before, your two-year-old will surely let you know. You aren't raising an angel. But then, by now you probably realize that you aren't exactly ready to be measured for your halo yet, either.

Peanut Butter and Jelly Sandwiches

*I*t's common knowledge. A writer should write about what she knows. And what I know about is peanut butter and jelly sandwiches. If you think there's not much to write about when it comes to peanut butter and jelly sandwiches, your taste buds have not been educated to the finer points of "PB and J Cuisine" as defined by my experts.

Take the bread . . . two slices . . . perfectly matched . . . preference for white . . . no bits of wheat or other suspicious-looking particles . . . no heels . . . no holes. It must not be too fresh. Fresh bread may be great for "skinning" the crust off and making those yummy dough balls, but it won't stand up to the peanut butter scene. On the other hand, bread from the bakery outlet store is sure to be classified as "too hard."

There was a time when any brand of peanut butter would have been suitable. Now, peanut butter must be low in sugar and salt. It must be creamier and peanuttier. The list of ingredients on the side must have a majority of words that don't have to be interpreted by a dietitian, and the jar must have a thirty-five-cent coupon on the back. Oh. It should also come fairly close to tasting like peanut butter.

Spreading the peanut butter takes practice and talent. The best peanut butter spreaders sweep each slice of bread with one masterful stroke of the knife. With peanut butter on each slice, the jelly will ooze out the sides better and won't make the bread soggy.

Choose a jelly that matches the carpet and is easy to remove from walls and floors. Glob a generous portion of jelly on one of the slices, place the slices together, and cut with a sharp, serrated knife on the diagonal . . . twice for toddlers. Serve on a saucer with a glass of milk, fruit wedges and a smile.

According to my experts, there's only one way to eat a peanut butter and jelly sandwich. Hold the crust edges with both hands and take the first bite from the middle, working your way in so the jelly spreads evenly on both sides of your mouth. Wipe the sticky part on your shirt when you're done. This will attract the best kinds of bugs when it's time to go back outside to play. It also brings out a good assortment of inside bugs if you have to stay in the house.

I'll take their word for it. You see, I make the sandwiches. I don't eat them.

don't come in here! Mom's throwing spagetti!

A Child is a Wonderful Thing

There are grown-ups. And there are children. I'm what they call a grownup. But I like children better. Children are. . . well . . . children. They work hard at goofing around. They sit at the edge of puddles and squeeze black, oozy mud between their toes. They say they're six-and-a-half-going-on-seven because they can hardly wait for more life to arrive. They dash toward time with an eager embrace and a slobbery kiss instead of trying to squirm free from its thorny grasp.

Children find joy in simple things . . . like the tickle of a yellow dandelion on their necks . . . a grape popsicle . . . the silky softness of a rabbit's fur . . . and the sight of an angleworm on a rainy sidewalk.

Children welcome challenges. Who can peel the largest patch of skin from a sunburned body? Who can skip a rock three times on the surface of a lake? Who can count the stars?

Children take the guesswork out of human relations. They're not stingy with their feelings. When you smile at them, they smile back. When they're sad or hurt or afraid, they cry on the outside. When somebody takes their favorite toy, they don't stop to analyze it. They just get it back.

Children don't know about "can't." In spite of bumps, bruises, scrapes and broken bones, they keep picking themselves up until they've mastered walking, riding a bike, skateboarding, or whatever else in the world interests them. To children, failure is a teacher.

Children are believers. They make wishes when they blow out the candles. They close their eyes and throw pennies into fountains and cast their dreams at the first star to appear in the vast evening sky. They search for four-leaf clovers. They think they won't get a sunburn.

Children are forgiving. They can't be bothered with nursing grudges. One moment, they dub you "the meanest human bean in the world," the next they offer to be your best friend.

Children bend. They haven't made definite plans. They aren't square-fillers, watch-wearers, calendar-keepers or card carriers. The only moment they're interested in is this one. Let somebody else fret about yesterday and tomorrow.

Children are creative. They never walk if they can skip, hop, jump or run. They never talk if they can giggle, chatter or squeal. They never look if they can inspect or peek. They never smell if they can sniff. They live life with zest and gusto.

Children are loving. They're ready to deliver two or three mooshy kisses for every one they receive. A hug fixes anything.

Children are optimistic. They think they can walk to Grandma's house. They think they can save their allowance and buy a Corvette.

Children are understanding. They don't carry around an unwritten list of standards for other peoples' lives.

Children are curious. They have a million questions, from "Where does God live?" to "Do water skippers have muscles?"

Children are the genuine article . . . unprogrammed . . . unpredictable . . . underrated . . . and often, unappreciated until they are marching in step with the rank and file of the grown-up troops. Then, they look over their shoulders, reach for the lost magic that belongs to childhood and realize the truth.

Children are the best way to start people.

don't come in here! Mom's throwing spagetti!

Are We Having Fun Yet?

One of the truest equations is "crisis plus time equals humor." I don't mean the kind of crisis that involves the loss of life or limb. I'm referring to the little mishaps that plunk themselves down in the middle of a perfectly wonderful day and take possession of your sense of humor until the whole fiasco is just a memory. Then, as if by magic, the incident turns hilariously funny.

Any mother worth her refrigerator magnets has a few tales to tell. Like the time my son and our neighbor's daughter mixed two dozen eggs with a pile of sawdust and fed the mixture to every stuffed animal in the house. I can giggle now, but I wasn't smiling while the eggs were drying.

A friend of mine has a story I'm happy to report I've never been able to match. She devised a plan for keeping track of her three preschoolers while shopping. She connected herself to the two older children by tying long lengths of sewing elastic between her wrists and theirs. She imagined that she could hold the baby in one arm and actually have one free hand to shop.

Everything was going according to the plan until she and her ducklings approached an escalator. One child got on. The other took one look at the moving stairs and toddled off screaming in the other direction. Meanwhile, the baby panicked and started to wail.

I don't imagine you feel much like a stand-up comedian when you're stranded at the bottom of an escalator stretched between two lengths of elastic and listening to one of your children holler, "Get on, Mom!" while the other two are doing everything in their power to keep you from doing just that . . . all the while disaster is opening its jaws as lengths of elastic pull tighter and tighter in both directions.

Nobody knows which end of the elastic would have snapped first if it hadn't been for two concerned bystanders. The bystander at the top of the escalator scrambled down the up-going stairs, picked up the escalator-friendly child and kept the slack in the elastic loosened by continuing to hold the child while keeping one step ahead (or behind, whichever way you prefer to look at it) of the moving stairs. In the meantime, the other onlooker picked up the escaping screamer, transported him to the bottom of the escalator and got on it with him, along with his mother and the baby . . . like it or not. At last, mother and her unpredictable brood were reunited at the top of the escalator midst a flood of relieved tears.

The shopping trip was over. The trip down the escalator and to the car was made without fanfare . . . or elastic. A few weeks later, she had recovered and could tell her story . . . but only between peals of laughter.

Crisis plus time equals humor? Nobody knows the truth of that statement like a mother. That's why nurturing a sense of humor is possibly the best mental health insurance a mother can take out. After all, when you're immersed in the profession of endless surprises, a sense of humor is NOT optional equipment. It helps you reflect on the past with a smile and anticipate the future with a determination to meet whatever comes next.

Just keep telling yourself, "Someday, I'm going to laugh at this."

don't come in
here!
mom's throwing
spagetti!

Just for Today

Just for today, the petunias in the back yard were safe. No carrots were uprooted from the garden to serve as third base. Flattened patches of grass gathered a flicker of hope and stretched their matted blades to meet the sun. The rubber ducky in the wading pool swam alone on a sea of still water. Ants dared to emerge from their anthills and play on our sidewalk.

Just for today, I took a nap in the middle of the morning. My toothbrush wasn't suspiciously wet when I reached for it. I soaked in the bathtub for thirty minutes under a mountain of bubbles. I curled my eyelashes. I left my favorite tube of lipstick on the counter, and it was still there when I came back.

Just for today, I didn't have to rescue any little plastic action figures from a watery grave in the toilet bowl. No globs of toothpaste appeared in the sink.

Just for today, no honey dripped down the sides of the cupboard. No puddles of grape Kool-Aid appeared on the counter. The refrigerator door was shut more than it was open. Nobody asked if they could make chocolate pudding. The jar of peanut butter stayed behind the cupboard door.

Just for today, the car stayed in the garage. No bicycles turned up with flat tires. Nobody asked for a motorcycle.

Just for today, no more towels disappeared. The ones in the closet stayed in a neat stack. The piles of clean laundry weren't replaced by piles of dirty laundry. No wadded up socks appeared in the living room. No muddy sneakers were found on the lawn.

Just for today, nobody asked, "What's for dinner?" No new fingerprints appeared on the windows and walls. I had time to dust the furniture, vacuum and clean a closet. The criss-cross marks left by the vacuum were visible for hours. Nobody hid a stash of chocolate chips underneath the couch.

Just for today, I listened to classical music. I read chapters from *Life and Death in Shanghai* instead of *The Cat in the Hat*. I played Bach on the piano instead of monitoring two hours of practicing. I called a friend and talked for twenty minutes straight.

Just for today, I watched the news without getting up once. I lived by the law of accomplishment instead of the law of interruptions.

Just for today, I baked cookies and got to eat the first one. I ate five more and called it dinner. I fertilized and watered the remaining houseplant and asked for its forgiveness for past wrongs. I encouraged it to hang in there for just a few more years.

Just for today, there were no arguments to settle. Nobody said things weren't fair. Nobody needed a Band-Aid. Nobody had to clean their room before they could go out to play.

Just for today, I was calm and refined. I heard the refrigerator hum and the clocks tick. I heard my brain formulating intelligent, adult ideas.

Just for today, I didn't run out of milk.

Just for today, my husband took the children fishing.

I'm Not A Housewife

I used to merely bristle at the title "Housewife." No more. Since our family bought a house with fourteen rooms, I've crossed the threshold into militancy.

The trouble with being married to a house is the one-sided communication. A house won't listen to reason. It insists on having its own wall-to-wall way.

Talk about marital problems. While one room is whining, "Wash my walls and baseboards," another is pining away for a new color scheme.

Just when I get the walls cleaned up, the kitchen floor shrieks, "Get that soggy lettuce off me!" Then all the carpets start pleading for a shampoo. Even the windows demand to be washed.

Have you ever tried to talk back to a house? The silent treatment can go on for years.

It's embarrassing being married to a house. People ask questions like, "Do you work?"

What do I look like? A lounge chair? A better question might be, "Do you know any mothers who DON'T work? Perhaps they think the kids and I spend our days hibernating in cocoons and emerge at night to dinner on the table, stacks of clean laundry and a potty-trained two-year-old. The answer is yes . . . I work!

There's another thing. Whenever I fill out a form and write in "Housewife" as my profession, I discover I have to leave the rest of the blanks empty. It's as if the term itself makes me as inanimate as the house is.

I'd just like to know where I was when the papers were drawn up and signed that wedded me to a house in the first place. One day I was a woman in love. The next thing I knew, a house had lassoed me and staked its claim.

I've lived with lots of houses on a trial basis and seen thousands more. Maybe I'm just fickle, but I have yet to be introduced to one I wanted to share a marriage license with. The very idea of tying the knot with an address makes me feel like crawling under a lampshade.

I've talked it over with my other husband. He understands. He's not interested in competing in a love triangle with a set of blueprints, either. He says house and I can't possibly make a go of it on our own. We can't even make the payments on each other. Not only that. He says house and I don't have much in common. He says I'm much too well-rounded to be stuck with such a square. Besides, he says he wants me all to himself.

Well, that settles it.

Therefore, I, Renee Hawkley, do solemnly renounce the title of "Housewife." Furthermore, let it be known by any persons who may feel inclined to refer to me as a "Housewife" that they should prepare to hear a long and rehearsed lecture on the need for the term to be deleted from the English language.

don't come in here! Mom's throwing spaghetti!

Pennies in the Soap Dish

Not every household has twenty-seven pennies in the soap dish. Ours hasn't always had them, either. Come to think of it, if you haven't visited us recently, you might have a few questions. Not to worry. I can explain everything.

About the pennies. My daughter, Janette (7), had to wash them. She says they were dirty. That's because a couple of summers ago, somebody in the house with twenty-seven pennies to spare threw them out the bedroom window, and they landed in a flower bed. Unfortunately, they failed to germinate and sprout into penny trees, and yesterday Ethan (10) discovered the buried treasure in the flower bed and gave them to Janette, and that's why we have pennies in the soap dish.

You might wonder what our cat, Tigger, is doing with a bandage tied around his head. Well, Tigger and Spice, the cat next door, are NOT best friends. The only thing they agree on is that birds don't belong on our property. Unfortunately, Tigger is smaller and a little less cunning, so when Tigger and Spice tangle, Tigger always loses. Last time he came home with a bloody head. Hence, the bandage.

Next, you may wonder why all the wastebaskets are on the counters and chests of drawers instead of on the floor, where wastebaskets should be. Well, it's because I'm babysitting a pair of eight-month-old twins, and all the goodies in the wastebaskets are just what eight-month-old twins who just learned to crawl love to play with best.

What are the ice cream containers of rocks doing on the porch? Actually, they've been there for the better part of a year, waiting for the day when they can have rose petals, feathers, and a sprinkle of sand added for rose petal stew.

So, you noticed the rug on the piano bench. It's there because nobody, but nobody likes to practice the piano on an old, hard bench, and the rug is one of those soft, homemade "Grandma made it" things that makes sitting and playing the piano a pleasure.

Yes, there are rubber bands scattered all over the driveway. When the boys go out on their early morning paper routes, they drop rubber bands and "forget" to pick them up when they get home.

Why is there a pile of games in the hall? Frankly, because there just isn't room for them in the closet until someone who has a little more time than I do rearranges the shelves so they will fit.

And what about the laundry basket full of clean, white socks in the laundry room? Well, the job everybody in the house hates the most is matching socks, so we save it for people who mess up, and lately everybody has been relatively well behaved. It's a sorry situation when a mother has to hope that someone will act up fairly soon so she won't have to match the socks herself.

I suppose that brings me to the question I know you've been dying to ask. You want to know why a woman of reasonable intelligence and maturity is wearing a white barrette with little duckies on the side to hold her hair out of her eyes. That's easy. It's because the pink one with the elephants doesn't match my outfit.

Mothers Can't Get Sick

I 'm sick. There should be a law against mothers getting sick. It's not like you can call in and take the day off. Personally, I don't need this kind of proof that I'm indispensable. I already know that survival on this planet would be impossible without air, sunshine, soil and mothers.

This job demands the health of an astronaut. There are simply no allowances for little interruptions like migraine headaches, appendicitis attacks or even mild cases of the hiccups.

I knew I was sick when I jumped up to turn off the alarm this morning and my stomach stayed in bed. "I think I have the flu," I told my husband, holding my head and crumbling back between the sheets.

"Oh, no. Not that," he said.

"Do I have a fever?"

"Feels like it. You'd better stay in bed. I have to leave early, but the kids can take care of things, can't they?"

"Would that be a multiple choice question or true and false?" I mumbled. "No matter. Either way, we're not prepared for the answer."

So starts the day. My husband gets up, takes a shower and gets ready for work. The kids come in one by one to ask what's for breakfast. One by one, I direct them to the corn flakes and toaster. One by one, they come to report that Janette spilled the milk. One by one, I tell them to wipe it up.

"Mom, do we still have to practice the piano, since we know it will disturb your headache?" asked Anthony.

"Yes, you still have to practice . . . just don't pound on the keys."

"But, Mom . . ." he says.

The house and all the systems in it begin to disintegrate when a mother is laid up in bed. And the smell. It's something akin to grape jelly, moldy laundry and cat litter that's a little heavy on the cat part and a little light on the litter part.

Errands don't get run. The full cartons of milk in the refrigerator turn to empty cartons on the counter. Teenage drivers run out of gas because Mom didn't fill the tank, car pools have to be revamped and appointments have to be canceled.

And have you noticed? There's something about a mother being sick that makes the toilet run over.   It's as if the toilet comes out in open rebellion with, "If she's throwing up, so am I!"

Eventually, the flu and the day pass away. Daddy comes home with two of those cardboard pizzas that were on sale at the supermarket. It's not homemade chicken soup, but at this point, who's fussy?

Poor man. His heart is in the right place. He supervises dinner and the dishes, scrapes the clumps of toothpaste off the carpet, mops up the bathroom floor, finishes the bedtime rituals with the kids and drags into the bedroom with the look of a basset hound in mourning.

"Is there any chance you'll feel better by morning?"

"Don't worry. I'll be better tomorrow if it kills me."

Don't Come in Here! Mom's Throwing Spaghetti!

*P*atience. There's that word again. It bothers me. When I'm not wishing I had more of it, I'm wondering why I keep losing the little I have. Getting patient takes too long. Iwant patience, and I want it now.

At least I know I'm in the right profession for acquiring it. There isn't a job anywhere that offers more chances for learning patience than mothering. Even neurosurgeons and high school basketball coaches get to go home after a hard day's night and leave their nerve-grinding work at the office. Not mothers.

A mother's patience gets wrung out and strung out on a never-ending clothesline of surprises. The variety covers everything from cleaning a bowl of soggy cat food out of the vacuum cleaner because one of your children tried to vacuum it up to trying to keep a fragile temper from shattering when a teenager calls at two a.m. asking if he can break his midnight curfew. Still, some mothers seem to have patience the rest of us only dream about.

I ask you. What's so hard about keeping just a sprinkle of poise when things don't go smoothly? It should be easy. All you do is nothing.

I asked one of my patient friends, Melody, if she could give me some pointers. She reminded me that mothers don't usually see each other behind closed doors, and then she told me her story.

One evening, Melody prepared a spaghetti dinner for her family. After setting the meal on the table, she called each member of the family and sat down to wait for them to appear. Five minutes passed. Nobody came. The spaghetti began to cool. Melody started heating up.

She called each member of the family a second time. Five minutes passed. Nobody came. The spaghetti got colder. Melody got warmer.

She called each one a third time and waited again. The spaghetti got even colder, and Melody got hot. When a couple of her teenage daughters finally sauntered into the dining room to take their places, they were too late. Melody had boiled over. She flung fistfuls of cold spaghetti at them and only came to her senses when they dashed out of the room shouting to the rest of the family, "Don't come in here! Mom's throwing spaghetti!"

Reassurance. That's what this story gives me. Reassurance and courage to start a new day, knowing that others have been and will be exasperated and angry and frustrated at times, too . . . just like me.

Where's The Thing-a-ma-jig?

I have a lot of important things to think about. Sometimes I get to thinking of so many important things at once that I can't coordinate my brain with my mouth.

Just yesterday, I asked one of my sons to bring me the thing-a-ma-jig from the bedroom.

"What thing-a-ma-jig?"

"You know what I mean. It's right next to the do-whappee."

"Which bedroom is the do-whappee in?" he asked.

"I mean the bathroom. It's on the diller in the bathroom."

"What diller?"

"You know. The thinger."

"What does it look like?"

"Don't get smart with me. It looks like itself. Come to think of it, it looks a lot like a wha-cha-ma-call-it."

"What does a wha-cha-ma-call-it look like?"

"Now listen here, Anthony. I don't like your tone of voice. It looks like a regular kind of wha-cha-ma-call-it, of course."

"My name isn't Anthony."

"What do you mean, your name isn't Anthony?"

"My name is Ethan."

"Oh . . . well . . . I guess you're right. Listen. If I've told you once, I've told you a thousand times. Don't listen to what I SAY. Listen to what I MEAN."

"Mom, why don't you ask somebody else to get your thing-ma-jig for you. I'll call Kyle to do it."

"No. Kyle is over at you-know-who's. Go upstairs and get who-jer."

"Who-jer?"

"Yes. Who-jer."

"Mom. Which who-jer do you mean?"

"I don't care. Just send somebody."

I ask you. Have you ever sent YOUR son for who-jer and actually had who-jer show up? Me, neither.

So, I had to go get the thing-a-ma-jig myself. It's a good thing I did.

A bunch of who-jers had been in the bathroom dumping wha-cha-ma-call-it all over the diller, and I was able to discover their shenanigans just in time to side-track a disaster.

Well. They didn't get away with it. I tracked the culprits down while the trail was fresh and made them clean the whole mess up.

I just don't know about these kids of mine. Where do they get their brains?

don't come in
Here!
Mom's Throwing
Spagetti!

Musings of a Mother on a Good Day

As a confirmed mother of eight, I can't get a letter to Ann Landers from an Illinois woman out of my mind. She and her husband have chosen to remain childless because "our planet has become overpopulated, polluted, drug-crazy, crime-ridden, and war-laden." She asked Ann to rerun an article written by a discouraged father entitled "Musings of a Good Father on a Bad Day."

The woman from Illinois and the discouraged father say the world is already in a big enough mess as it is. Why bring more children into it, especially considering the expenses and challenges of parenting?

I suppose they have a point. Still, if I had the decision to make again, I'd close my eyes and jump into the uncertain world of parenthood like an eager parachutist.

Don't tell me I'm not being logical. I already know. While some childless couples are, as the discouraged father recounts, "stretched out, relaxing around swimming pools in Florida and California," we're applying sunscreen to little noses and teaching a two-year-old to put her face in the water.

While they're "trotting off to Europe like fools, with money to spend, time to enjoy themselves and nothing to worry about," we're saving dimes, quarters, nickels and pennies in a cider jug for a trip to Disneyland. While they're enjoying the opera, my husband and I are attending an eighth-grade band concert where the clarinet section squeaks and our own "star" maintains second chair in the trumpet section. Only six more payments, and the trumpet will be ours.

While they're enjoying a romantic evening in an Italian restaurant, we're patronizing the drive-thru at McDonald's while on our way to a Little League game. While they're getting facelifts, we're dashing to the emergency room with a child who fell over his brother's bike and broke his arm.

While they're "wrestling the guests for the olives in their martinis," we're spreading peanut butter and jelly. While they're off to the movies, we're rolling the camera for the premiere performance of "Eensy weensy spider" by our toddler.

While they're buying BMW's, we're writing checks for college tuition. While their holiday seasons are brimming with peace on earth, ours are chaotic and budget wrenching.

Why DO parents choose to spend so many years passing the torch of life instead of running with it themselves? If the world goes down the tubes and up in smoke, what will it matter that we invested our time, energy and money in the next generation while others invested in themselves?

I regret that I can't present a clear answer. I suppose it has something to do with optimism. Perhaps we parents bank on the idea that as long as there are children in the world, there's still hope. Perhaps we choose to be parents because we like spending our lives on something that will last longer than we do. Maybe we think that in spite of the doom-and-gloom-sayers, the children will help us find a way where there is no way.

Personally, my reason isn't that sophisticated. There's just something downright comforting about knowing that I'll always have little arms around my neck.

Technology on the Loose

I'm keeping a few secrets from my kids. One of them is that I took a class called "typing" in high school. It was there that I learned to type, "All good men should come to the aid of their country" and other statements of profound wisdom on a typewriter that didn't have an ON/OFF switch. Not only that, all the typewriter did was print little black letters and numbers on a piece of paper. It didn't correct mistakes, delete phrases, go back to the main menu, print three copies, correct my spelling, insert sentences, change fonts or save my work on a diskette. It didn't have graphics, and it didn't turn into a video game when I got tired of typing the boring stuff.

The fact that technology is taking over doesn't worry me so much. The thing that scares me is that children are the only people who understand it. Just follow a kid around for a day. Any kid. Then try to explain how he got all his information.

These days, even the most sheltered toddlers know how to use the TV remote and program the VCR. By the time they turn three, they've graduated to dubbing tapes and playing Ms. PacMan, and by four, they're sending email. It's no wonder that a kindergarten child isn't exactly swept off her feet at the sight of the computer lab at school. Actually, computers are put in classrooms these days so that teachers can pick up a few tips from the kids on how to use them.

The difference between "our" generation and the new one is that "we" were raised with machines while "they" are being raised with technology. They have no problem mastering monitors, URL's or video games. However, it seems they have trouble getting the gist of the simple machinery lever action of an "Off" switch until they move out of their parents' home and have received their first electricity bill.

A washing machine is much too complicated for a child of normal IQ. Those who can handle setting the cycles and turning the machine on have difficulty adding the detergent, bleach and softener in the correct amounts and at the appropriate times.

Teaching a child how to load and operate a dishwasher takes even the most optimistic parent years of dedicated devotion, including repeated demonstrations. Children have similar difficulties with sewing machines, ovens and clothes dryers. However, microwaves are a snap. That's because a microwave is a technological advance, not a machine.

No. It doesn't make sense to me, either. There isn't a kid in America today who couldn't sit in the driver's seat of a Corvette and demonstrate the use of its computer panel. These are the same individuals who can't figure out how to operate the ripcord on a lawnmower.

Jigsaw Puzzle in the Wrong Box

There's this thing I've noticed about wise people. Their wisdom didn't sprinkle out of heaven like cool, summer rain. They got it by taking crash courses they didn't sign up for. Take my wise, young friend, Diane. She qualifies as being young in my book because she isn't a veteran of teenagers yet. She qualifies as being wise (in anybody's book) because she's been mining big nuggets of wisdom out of the deep and scary mine fields of adversity with some pretty old-fashioned tools; faith, sweat, and dedication.

Her fifth child, a baby boy named Logan, was born with special needs, and the family has, with love and devotion, made many life-altering adaptations. I see Diane often, and I marvel at how she continues to balance all the aspects of being a "regular" mom with Logan's ongoing and constant needs.

Many people ask her how she manages, and she modestly admits she doesn't have any secrets. However, she does tell a personal story that helps to shape many of her days and gives her strength. With her permission, I would like to retell it.

Diane loves jigsaw puzzles. However, since jigsaw puzzles and being the mother of preschoolers don't exactly mesh, she has disciplined herself to do only one puzzle per year. One year, after carefully shopping for the puzzle with the most pieces and the most captivating picture, she brought it home, set up the card table, and began working on it, using the picture on the box as a frequent point of reference.

As jigsaw puzzles go, this one got off to a slow start. The normal strategies didn't work, and it soon became apparent that the puzzle pieces were no match for the picture on the box. Frustrated that the puzzle company couldn't match puzzle pieces with boxes, she considered returning it and requesting a puzzle that wasn't flawed.

However, after working hard at assembling bits and pieces of the puzzle, she noticed that hints of the unknown picture had begun to reveal themselves.

It isn't hard to guess the end of the story. She decided to finish the puzzle without the advantage of the picture on the box. Even though the process was much harder and the final product much different from her initial expectations, her satisfaction at finishing it surpassed that of any previous puzzle she had worked on, and the picture turned out to be even more beautiful than the one she had initially selected.

Adversity is an unyielding taskmaster. No matter how careful we are in making life's choices, most of us find that we are working on puzzles and challenges that we have no "picture on the box" to go by.

Oh, sure, we can consider taking our puzzles back to God and demanding a refund or at least an explanation, but unfortunately, many of life's puzzles are nonrefundable and nonexplainable. When it comes right down to it, we can either pick up the next piece and work with study, diligence, and heart to discover how and where it fits, or we can pick a convenient scapegoat to blame, throw our hands up in frustration, and quit.

The choice is ours.

Just Don't Act Like A Mother

Recently, my teenage boys paid me the ultimate compliment of allowing me to go shopping with them. There were conditions. I had to bring my purse. The one with the checkbook. One of them said, "If you come, you can't act like a mother."

"What do you mean by that?" I asked.

"You know. Don't touch us," one of them offered.

"Yeah," piped in the second, "and don't talk like you love us or tell us to stand up straight or that."

"Just don't look at us," the third added.

"OK," I said. "Let me get this straight. I can come if I don't touch you, talk to you, or look at you."

"That's pretty much it," they agreed.

Well. Who could turn down an offer like that?

So, off we went to the mall in search of p.e. sweats and a couple of pairs of shoes.

If I may take the opportunity to boast, I behaved myself to perfection. Eyes straight ahead. Mouth shut. Hands to myself. The perfect example of apathy. A few educated shoppers may have guessed that I was the mother of these "dudes" by virtue of having teenagers of their own. But they didn't get any hints from me.

We bought what we came for and then split up to do some independent browsing. The boys went to *Pederson's*, a sporting goods store, and I headed for a sale at *Just Petites*, my favorite clothing shop.

"What does petite mean?" the youngest one asked.

"Short," said one of his older brothers. "It's a shop for short girls."

"Why don't they call it *Just Short*?" asked the first.

I shook my head, rolled my eyes and agreed to meet them at *Pederson's* in thirty minutes. Twenty minutes later, they had come back to find me at *Just Petites*.

"Mom, what's taking so long? We want to show you something," said one.

"Mom, come on. Somebody might see us' in here," said another.

"Alright, alright, I'm coming," I said.

In *Pederson's*, they directed me to the object of their affection . . . a hot pink snowboard. They looked me straight in the eyes and asked, "Isn't it great, Mom?"

"You're looking at me," I said. "People might get ideas."

"Come off it, Mother," another one said as he grabbed my arm and pulled me in the direction of the skateboards. "You gotta see this 'rad' board."

"You're touching me," I reminded him. "What if someone thinks we're related?"

"Mom, get real. This is important."

The other boy called me from the ski department, loud enough for everyone in the store to hear. "Mom, come look at these skis! They're the best!"

"Not so loud," I said as I sauntered over to the ski department, "and don't call me Mom in public. It's embarrassing."

On the way to the car, I asked them if I had passed the test well enough to be invited to go shopping again.

"Sure, Mom," they agreed. "Except you acted a little strange in *Pederson's*."

"What are you smiling for?" one of them asked.

"You didn't tell me I couldn't smile," said I.

Bring Back the Long Gone Olden Days

*M*y husband and I went to school in the olden days. Just ask our teenagers.

"Things were EASY in your century," they say.

I hate to admit it, but they're right. Way back then, we were a pretty sheltered bunch.

Way back then, sex was the word with the little line beside it that you wrote "M" or "F" on. Drugs were what you picked up at the corner drug store when you had bronchitis. Abortion was one of those "dictionary" words you looked up behind closed doors and NEVER said out loud. The name Madonna was associated with virginity.

The worst TV violence was when Wally gave The Beave a bloody nose. The only movies that played at the local theater were for family viewing. School was a safe place from the bad stuff.

What happened? And how did it all change so fast? Everything just seemed to creep in when nobody was paying attention.

It's tempting to blame the whole mess on television, too many or not enough government programs, the school board, teachers, rock music, the neighbors' kids, those "other" parents or just the system. After all, blaming has been on the charts as one of the top five things for human beings to do ever since Adam took a bite out of the apple and said, "Eve made me do it."

The trouble with blaming is that it's like continually shuffling a deck of cards. The movement suggests progress, takes up time and confuses things, but it doesn't move the game along. Unfortunately, in this game, if each player doesn't stop shuffling, take charge of the cards in his own hand and get into the game, the upcoming generation may very likely fold.

I'm a parent and a big fan of children. That counts. I can't shoulder ALL the responsibility, but I can make a positive difference in a few places. I can do my best to keep track of where my own kids are, what they're doing and who they're spending time with. Anyone with teenagers knows this is a classic example of "easier said than done." Still, it appears to me that parents who pay the premiums of time and caring seem to be holding the best-paying insurance policies.

Oh, sure. Our kids object at our wanting to know where, why, what, how, and who they are with at all times.

"Mom, you guys are too strict!," "Dad, no other parents make their kids do that!," "It isn't fair!," "Mom and Dad, get REAL!," and the very tired, "You don't understand!"

We understand better than they think. We once had parents who were too strict, who weren't fair, and who didn't understand. They insisted on knowing where, why, what, how, and who we were with at all times.

When we became parents, our parents got real . . . real wise, that is. The best part of the long-gone-olden days are the memories of parents who cared.

don't come in here! Mom's throwing spagetti!

Mothers are Y2K Compatible

(December, 1999)

*T*he last grains of sand cling to the sides of the 20th century hourglass. Are the world's computers ready? We'll soon know. In the meantime, mothers are. Mothers are Y2K compatible!

When computers register two zeroes on January 1st, 2000, mothers will continue wiping little noses, reading bedtime stories and kissing it better. Granted, they may have to be creative if grocery stores are out of Kleenex and the light switch won't produce a roomful of light because computers don't know how to go over a speed bump. Mothers specialize in going over speed bumps.

Mothers will continue to wash clothes, run errands and get meals on the table. So maybe the washer and dryer won't work, the service stations won't have gas, the stove won't heat and the restaurants are closed. Mothers will improvise, just like their great-grandmothers who survived World War II and the Great Depression.

They will continue to get up at 3:00 a.m. for the baby's last feeding, wait up for a teenager who is out past curfew, comfort a sick child in the middle of the night and wake paper boys up so they can deliver their papers on time. A little thing like the turn of the century will have little effect on mothers and their abilities to manage the lack of sleep.

They will continue to crochet afghans for grandchildren and listen to daily triumphs and tragedies of their offspring. They will continue to kneel by the beds of their little ones and listen to their prayers. They will continue to sing lullabies and give hugs and pick up clutter and spread peanut butter and jelly. They will continue teaching values, monitoring homework, packing lunches and paying for music lessons.

When their children are hurt, sick or afraid, mothers will continue to dry tears and cry tears. They will continue to bring new life into the world and give much of their lives in service to their families, just like they have been doing for ever-so-much-longer than computers have been around.

I'm not too worried about Y2K. Mothers are ready.

Somebody Said

(Reprinted in *Reader's Digest*)

Somebody said a mother is an unskilled laborer . . . somebody never gave a squirmy infant a bath.

Somebody said it takes about six weeks to get back to normal after you've had a baby . . . somebody doesn't know that once you're a mother, normal is history.

Somebody said a mother's job consists of wiping noses and changing diapers . . . somebody doesn't know that a child is much more than the shell he lives in.

Somebody said you learn how to be a mother by instinct . . . somebody never took a three-year-old shopping.

Somebody said being a mother is boring . . . somebody never rode in a car driven by a teenager with a driver's permit.

Somebody said teachers, psychologists and pediatricians know more about children than their mothers . . . somebody hasn't invested her heart in another human being.

Somebody said if you're a "good" mother, your child will "turn out" . . . somebody thinks a child is like a bag of plaster of Paris that comes with directions, a mold and a guarantee.

Somebody said being a mother is what you do in your spare time . . . somebody doesn't know that when you're a mother, you're a mother ALL the time.

Somebody said "good" mothers never raise their voices . . . somebody never came out the back door just in time to see her child wind up and hit a golf ball through the neighbor's kitchen window.

Somebody said you don't need an education to be a mother . . . somebody never helped a fourth grader with his math.

Somebody said you can't love the fifth child as much as you love the first . . . somebody doesn't have five children.

Somebody said a mother can find all the answers to her child-rearing questions in the books . . . somebody never had a child stuff beans up his nose.

Somebody said the hardest part of being a mother is labor and delivery . . . somebody never watched her "baby" get on the bus for the first day of kindergarten.

Somebody said a mother can do her job with her eyes closed and one hand tied behind her back . . . somebody never organized seven giggling Brownies to sell cookies.

Somebody said a mother can stop worrying after her child gets married . . . somebody doesn't know that marriage adds a new son or daughter-in-law to a mother's heartstrings.

Somebody said a mother's job is done when her last child leaves home . . . somebody never had grandchildren.

Somebody said a mother should forget a wayward child and get on with her life . . . somebody doesn't know much about the power of God and love and prayer and patience and miracles.

Somebody said being a mother is a side dish on the plate of life ... somebody doesn't know what fills you up.

Somebody said your mother knows you love her, so you don't need to tell her . . . somebody isn't a mother.

Commandments for Raising Teens

*T*hou shalt let thy teenager go. Thou shalt let him go to football games, movies, dances, debate tournaments and band performances. Thou shalt let him go in thy best car, which has a full tank of gas. Thou shalt not misplace thy car keys at any time. Thou shalt consider installing revolving doors at all points of departure from thy home so thy teenager's comings and goings may be executed efficiently.

*T*hou shalt not talk to, touch, or look in thy teenager's direction while in a public place.

*T*hou shalt not tell thy teenager what to wear. Thou shalt not help thy teenager shop for clothes or suggest brand names, styles or colors. Thou shalt avoid the topic of correct sizes at all costs.

*T*hou shalt provide much food. Thou shalt stock thy refrigerator and cupboards with many perishables. Thou shalt not count oatmeal, cans of soup, vegetables or fruits as food.

*T*hou shalt not be thy teenager's pal. Thou shalt not try to look, act, talk, or dress like unto thy teenager.

*T*hou shalt not exaggerate stories of thy childhood struggles or fame. Thou shalt not continue to repeat stories about thy childhood more than once a year.

*T*hou shalt not ground thy teenager. If thy teenager should ever need to be corrected . . . according to thy teenager, this is highly unlikely . . . thou shalt realize that being grounded is extremely difficult for thy teenager, but having thy teenager grounded for any length of time whatsoever will prove to be cruel and unusual punishment to all other members of the family.

*T*hou shalt love thy teenager as thyself, not expecting thy teenager to be just like thee. Thou shalt not impose thy favorite hobbies and talents upon thy teenager in a forceful manner but shalt allow thy teenager space to develop individual interests.

*T*hou shalt guard thy tongue. Thou shalt not bow down unto the powers of yelling, belittling, or sarcasm. Thou shalt speak unto thy teenager as thou would have him speak unto thee, using words of respect and encouragement. Thou shalt restrain thyself from saying, "I told you this would happen," or "This may come as a surprise, but there are a few things you don't know."

*T*hou shalt do thy very best, show confidence and trust in thy teenager, pray a lot, count thy blessings that thy teenager is keeping thee young, and thank thy lucky stars for the inspiring, faith-promoting words, "And it came to pass."

Thoroughly
Modern Mother

*T*he other day, one of my teenage
sons and I were discussing a school
friend of his. I asked him to tell me about her family since
she had invited him to a party at their home.

He got off to a great start, but then added, "Well, Mom
. . . her mom's not like you."

"What do you mean by that?" I countered.

"Well," he grimaced, "she's just different."

"How different?"

"Well, not really different. Just different."

"If you can't tell me HOW she's different, you can't
go to the party," I came back at him.

"Well, Mom. She's a . . . well, a . . . a . . . modern
mother."

I know a low blow when I feel one. I had just been
labeled "old fashioned" by my teenager, and I'm smart
enough to recognize the truth when I hear it.

I suspect there are several reasons I fit the old-fashioned
mold. For one thing, I can rattle off the ingredients for
pie crust, and I even put them together occasionally. I
like going to church, and I even sing in the choir.

The threadbare Daffy Duck towel in the master
bathroom doesn't match the decor, and I still put a drop
of Ivory Liquid on my kids' tongues whenever I hear big,
bad words like "shut up" come out of their mouths.

My idea of living dangerously is driving to the

42

grocery store without wearing my seatbelt. I don't work out at the fitness center, and I don't own a French leotard.

If all the above isn't enough, I think a family should eat together at least once a day, and I like baking cookies.

All is not lost, however. I remember thinking my Mom was out of step with the times when I was a teenager, too. She wore a housedress and apron every day and didn't own a pair of jeans. Store-bought bread was a treat we seldom experienced.

She devoted every Tuesday to ironing. Her makeup consisted of a tube of lipstick and was reserved for Sundays. She was always canning fruits and vegetables. She curled her hair with bobby pins while the "in" crowd was using brush rollers. She even put Mentholatum on her lips every night at bedtime.

You won't hear me complaining about being raised by an old-fashioned mom now. As a matter of fact, I consider it one of the greatest privileges of my life and hope my own kids take my point of view in a few years.

I suppose we are allowed new perspectives on motherhood once in awhile. I like one adopted by one of my preschoolers. After his Sunday School teacher had come for a short visit, he asked, "Isn't she a nice mother?"

I explained that she wasn't a mother yet. He replied, "Yes she is, Mom. I saw her checkbook and keys in her purse."

Whoever said, "The hand that rocks the cradle is the hand that rules the world" needs to update his quote a little. It should read, "The hand that holds the checkbook and keys is the hand that rules the world."

I figure that's one point grandmothers, old-fashion mothers, and modern mothers can agree on.

Graduation Day

(Printed in *Reader's Digest*)

I never thought it would come to this. Our oldest son is graduating from high school. The eighteen-year-old whirlwind is about to relocate.

One day soon, I will enter his "untouchable" room. I expect to find out once and for all what causes that persistent smell—an intriguing aroma best described as something between sweaty socks and peanut butter cups. I will rummage through the pile of whatever-it-is on his bed and launder the pair of matching sheets. I'll put them back on the bed just like they looked in the catalog I ordered them from. I'll put the matching pillowcase on the pillow, breathe a grateful sigh that the blanket his Grandma Thomas hand-quilted for him is still intact, and align the lengthwise part of the bedspread with the lengthwise part of the bed.

I will go through the stuffed bottom drawer of the chest and count the candy-bar wrappers. I will marvel that its owner has never had a cavity.

I will hide the weight set in the closet and examine several gouges in the walls made by one sports apparatus or the other. Yes, I know. It was an accident, Mom. With any luck, my husband and I will be able to fix most of them with spackling compound and a can of paint.

I will vacuum corners, scrub walls, disinfect mopboards and shine windows. I will confiscate, eradicate and eliminate all dust-ball families that have been breeding with the gum wrappers and dirty combs under the bed.

Then I'll organize the stamp collection and baseball cards for storage. I'll gather all the camera parts and put them in their little compartments in the camera case. I'll bag pairs of holey sneakers for the garbage can. Then I'll close the door, fully expecting to open it later to the organized sight I left behind.

It will be the dawn of a new day for me.

He won't be spending forty-five minutes morning and night running the hot water out of the shower. He won't be pulling my car out of the driveway just as I am about to use it.

He won't be phoning to see if tonight's curfew is the same as last week's. "Is there anything good to eat?" will be heard less. I won't holler "Turn it down!" so often.

No more complaints that I didn't get the shirts out of the dryer soon enough. No more expensive ties wadded up in the hamper. No more friends who favor me with a "Hi" only after the refrigerator, cupboards and freezer have been stripped of dip, chip and pizza.

No more hassle over haircuts. No more wondering whether he will wear his jeans out before they become high-waters. No more late-night waiting and worrying.

And no more looking up into those ocean-blue eyes that used to belong to a boy.

Maybe if I practice smiling enough, I will be convincing on graduation day. I don't want to spoil what he has pegged as the happiest day of his life.

It will be one of the saddest of mine.

What's in the Word "Family"?

*F*or appealing definitions, check out the newest one of family: a gathering of people who sleep under the same roof. As definitions go, it's as limp as a popped balloon.

It's true. Families have changed. But it'll take more than a dishrag definition and changing times to wring the heart out of the word family. Because family isn't just a word. It's the very soul of life that defies definition. It's the daily surprises . . . the ins and the outs . . . the adding and subtracting . . . the multiplying and dividing . . . the highs and the lows . . . the laughing and crying . . . the winning and the losing . . . the forgiving and forgetting. Family is what's left over when all the frills of life are taken away.

Take our family of ten. Six boys, two girls, a mom, a dad, two pianos, a goldfish, a couple of rabbits, a five-bedroom house and an odd assortment of miscellaneous. It's not exactly a typical family. But then, what exactly IS a typical family?

You can't fit a family into a definition like you'd pour Jello into a mold. Even if you could, it would never set up in perfect form according to a recipe.

One way to define what a family IS is by listing some of the things a family ISN'T. A family isn't the people who cook your food at the fast-food restaurant, your teacher or classmates at school, the caregivers at the

46

daycare center or the people who sit in the pew behind yours at church. A family isn't the actors on your favorite sit-com, the friends you eat lunch with, your dentist and his staff, the author of your most-beloved book or any number of other people with whom you have some passing or not-so-passing interaction.

A family is about genuine belonging. It's about acceptance and emotions and long-term connections and loving people anyway.

It's the sirloin steak of life, including bone, fat and gristle. It defines you. It's what's real. It's the escape from the outside. It's the people you practice how to be a human being with. And when you fail, you practice and practice and then practice some more.

A family is about marriage and mothers and fathers and children and grandparents and uncles and aunts and cousins. A family is a living, breathing, evolving thing. It's now. It's then. It's tomorrow. It's hours and days and months and years. It's what you go through with the people you care about. It's not just an obligation or a duty. It's a commitment. It's a timeless investment in life.

A family is about sacrifice and being there and sharing life with someone. It's about the sum adding up to more than the value of its individual parts. It's knowing that whatever happens, you're not alone, and neither are they. It's the worry and the new gray hairs and the letters and the phone calls. It's the joy of discovering that a Porsche isn't going to be big enough for your trip down the road of life.

Quite simply, a family is where you came from, where you are, and where you're going. Now, there's a definition I can look forward to sinking a set of dentures into.

Melody of Life

O ne way or another, children turn their parents into old people. Take my parents. Years ago, my husband and I turned them into grandparents. In a few days, our daughter and her husband will make great-grandparents out of them, and there's no denying that great-grandparents aren't exactly spring chickens.

My husband and I will then be living with a house full of sons who will be uncles. Even our nine-year-old daughter will be promoted to "Aunt Janette." That will make my husband a grandfather, and I will be a . . . a . . . a grandmother!

I was just getting used to being a mother-in-law, and now this. I do have a few well-earned gray hairs and plenty of good cookie recipes saved up and a great lap for sitting on and all that, but isn't a grandmother supposed to feel older?

The one sure thing about parenting is that nobody gets enough job seniority to master all the stages. Just when you think you have the perfect formula for potty training, you're fresh out of three-year-olds and floundering with bedtime strategies, report card surprises and teenagers who think a set of car keys should be permanent appendages to their fingers. Parenting is the most bona fide, trial and error, hands on, up close and personal, agony and ecstasy, pick yourself up and dust yourself off job in the world.

Nowhere is there greater joy or more thorough wringing of your hands and heart. Nowhere are there more miracles, and nowhere is there more mud.

Only yesterday, my husband and I were watching our first baby bouncing in his little "Johnny Jump-Up" that hung in the hall. Now, he's a college graduate who gets bristly stubble all over his face when he doesn't shave. The little girl with the deep dimples who used to reserve her special brand of smiles and kisses for her dad now saves them for our son-in-law.

As a child, I didn't notice the song of life when my own parents were singing the notes to me. And my husband and I have been so engrossed in the challenge of learning the musical score that, while we've been practicing it with our own children, we haven't appreciated it's rhythmic beauty.

Life has come full circle for us and our daughter, the expectant mother who not so long ago asked for nursery rhymes and bedtime stories. Now, she and her husband have begun their own harmony. The tempo and dynamics will be different, but the music . . . the music will be familiar to us and our own parents as well. It's ironic. Just when parents have learned to read the notes to their own little symphony, life's repeating song is transferred to the heads and hands and hearts of amateurs again.

This time around, her father and I will be watching and encouraging from a front row seat in the audience. This time, our job is to keep our hearts open and our mouths shut . . . letting go of our children so they'll hold on to us . . . sitting on our hands so the new conductors can freely interpret the music . . . and enjoying a new variation on a very old melody.

don't come in here! Mom's throwing Spagetti!

Watch Me, Mom

Some things about parents and their children make the leap from generation to generation. Like the fact that children never outgrow the need to share their skills and successes with their parents.

Our grandchildren, Rachel and Charles, demonstrated this during a holiday visit. Rachel needed to show her parents and grandparents why she is "the smartest girl" in her kindergarten class by reading the book, <u>Marvin K. Mooney, Will You Please Go Now?</u> She also needed to show off how each bathtub toy at Grandma's house works and how she can sit still while getting her bangs cut. Not to be outdone, Charles showed off his belly button, the colors red and yellow from a box of crayons and how fast he can eat a banana.

Recently my father, William Thomas, who has served Idaho citizens for over sixty years as a teacher, principal, superintendent of schools and philanthropist, received the prestigious Idaho School Boards Association Citizenship Award.

It was exciting for my mother, my sister, Shirlyn, and I to fly with him to Coeur d'Alene, where the award was presented. Hundreds of prominent people were to attend the banquet, including Idaho Senator Larry Craig. But one very important person wouldn't be there.

We got ready for the banquet in our motel room. As

Dad was straightening his tie in front of the mirror, he turned to Mother and softly said, with eyes glistening, "I wish my mother could be here to see me get this award."

And that's how it is and ever will be with children and the parents who love them.

Maybe I'm just a dreamer, but when Daddy stood at the podium to give a brief speech and receive his award, I'm pretty sure my Grandma Thomas was near, beaming with pride as her 89-year-old "little boy" received his standing ovation.